Stalker

Lucy Hamilton was born in Sheringham, Norfolk. Her mother was born in Paris and grew up in Toulouse (of Catholic and Jewish lineage) and her father grew up in Liverpool. She was joint recipient of the Poetry School Award 2006/7. Ten poems from her pamphlet *Sonnets for my Mother* have been translated into Arabic. In 2010 she became the first woman and first non-Muslim in the world to appear, by live satellite recording, reading her poems at the Havana Café, Mecca. She co-edits *Long Poem Magazine* and lives in Cambridge. In 2011 she co-judged the inaugural Cambridge University Benjamin Zephaniah Poetry Competition.

Also by Lucy Hamilton

Sonnets for my Mother (Hearing Eye, 2009)

Lucy Hamilton

Stalker

Shearsman Books

First published in the United Kingdom in 2012 by
Shearsman Books
50 Westons Hill Drive
Emersons Green
Bristol
BS16 7DF

Shearsman Books Ltd Registered Office
30–31 St. James Place, Mangotsfield, Bristol BS16 9JB
(this address not for correspondence)

www.shearsman.com

ISBN 978-1-84861-224-2

Copyright © Lucy Plowright Hamilton, 2012.
The right of Lucy Hamilton to be identified as the author
of this work has been asserted by her in accordance with the
Copyrights, Designs and Patents Act of 1988.
All rights reserved.

Acknowledgements
Some of these poems, or earlier versions of them, have previously
appeared in *Shearsman*, *Magma*, *Poetry Wales*, *Shadow Train*, *The Rialto*,
In the Company of Poets (ed. John Rety, Hearing Eye, 2003)
and *This Line Is Not For Turning: An Anthology of
Contemporary British Prose Poetry* (ed. Jane Monson,
Cinnamon Press, 2011).

My warmest thanks go to Mimi Khalvati for her ongoing
encouragement and inspirational classes, and to Linda Black for
her helpful comments and generous involvement throughout.
Special thanks to my husband John for his constant support.

Contents

1. Ghosts & Clochards

Feet	11
Ghost-riders	12
Tisane	13
Rue …	14
All Hallows	15
L'Heure du Déjeuner	16
Shadows	17
The Marseillaise	18
Clochard	19
The Concierge's Cat	20

2. Storms & Stations

Montparnasse — Rambouillet	23
His Letters Are in Pencil	24
The Light-Bearer	25
Tornado	26
Crazy Horse	27
What Men Did Not Read in Their Hearts	28
Dark Matters	29
Landmarks & Boundaries	30

3. Apparitions & Intimations

Algae Beds, Wyoming	33
Disturbances	34
On the Greyhound	35
On the Highway	36
The Christian Hostel for Men and Women	37
Warnings	38
Old Man	39
Aegean Sea	40
Cortège	41

4. Nightmares & Daymares

Nigg Bay, Aberdeen	45
Nazareth House	46
Sleep	47
Loons & Quines	48
Not Jenever/Not Friend	49
Absurd Nights	50

5. Rooms & Roads

Tempelhof	53
A Road in Berlin	54
Der Rote Stern Verlag	55
A Room in Northfield	56
Reservoir	57
On a Cliff at Hayle	58
Litany	59
The MAFF, Whitehall	60
Christian Street, Whitechapel	61
Flight	62

6. Death & Magic

The World Is a Swaying Lantern	65
Theories on the Origin of a Name	66
The Ferry	67
A Whiff of the Medieval	68
Gordon Gardens	69
The Chair	70
Wodnesdaeg	71
Gillingham to Gravesend	72
The Greasy Spoon	73
A Tale of Two (I)	74
A Tale of Two (II)	75
In a Street off Echo Square	76

7. Stalker

And the Sun Will Shine	79
Singing in the Rain	80
'Rose-bush' at My Window	81
Company	82
The Compulsion	83
Inside the Telephone Kiosk	84
Panda	85
Signet Ring	86

Notes   88

For Joanna,
and for Stefan

1. Ghosts & Clochards

Feet

The first morning I assume it's the result of an oversight from the night before. But the following morning and then the one after that I slowly begin to link my cousins' whispers with my coal-black feet. Eventually I have to ask Tante Annie what's going on. It started around the house, she says, gliding into their bedroom, standing over them like a zombie. Then into the girls' rambling room, climbing over the five beds, once even picking up little Katia before placing her back in her bed. One night they spotted me from an upstairs window playing *now you see me, now you don't* between the cypresses and poplars along the bridle-path. They followed me through the woods, down to the Garonne. "What did I look like?" I ask. "Just like in the films: eyes wide, arms outstretched." Late that night I sit on the edge of my bed cradling each foot in turn, trying to read its sole. Where does it want to go? Is it any part of *me* at all?

Ghost-riders

I'm attracted to the glow of the brazier, to the imagined camaraderie, to these low bridges beneath which the *clochards* apparently seek and find intimacy. Occasionally, strolling along in some reverie of my own, I'm alarmed by a sudden shout, or by a snatch of conversation flung by a squall of wind, like a flat leaf in my face. I glance up and see them shuffling around the fire, warming their hands, and smile at having been frightened. Today I can't see them at all. Voices reach my ears muffled in the thick milky mist that has reduced visibility to nil.

I don't proceed under the bridge—don't cross that line between the visible and the invisible, which is itself invisible. I remain on the edge, pushing my antennae into the heart of the dark. The smell is of sulphur not men. Nor meths. Nor chestnuts roasting in the shadow of the Eiffel Tower. I can sense their bodies, misshapen and clammy inside newspapers and rags. Bodies ravaged by neglect and premature aging. Mine is hard and young under the reversible green and gold cape my mother made for me. I stand on the edge—in between.

It begins as a low vibration, a disturbance in the sluggish air brushing my inner-ear. And now I can hear it, the lovely chug chug chug of a *remorqueur*. A friendly, comforting sound like that of an airplane reaching across the isolation of childhood insomnia. Chug chug chug. The mist is thinning but still hangs in a thick blanket over the Seine. If you filled a pint glass with river and mist it would look like Guinness. And now, as the invisible barge passes in front of me, I laugh out loud. For all I can see is a pair of erect bicycles moving along above the layer of mist, and I swear their ghost-riders wave back to me as I call out a greeting. I stare after them until they disappear, and then I too walk on, thinking of that other constellation: The Horse and the Rider—Rilke's *stars of the land of pain*.

Tisane

Tante Annie is teaching me recipes, telling me family histories. She pushes the leeks and garlic through the Moulie and onions sting our eyes as she fills in the details, corrects my French. Once a month she stays in bed sipping *tisane* while Oncle René receives his clients in the Louis Quinze salon. Each time I look out the window I recall her porcelain face, that hollow, jaundiced look. I envisage her tiny boy lying on the cobbles like a dropped doll.

Rue …

I'm walking blindfold, describing the road according to the fragrance of time of day and season, the odour of shop-fronts and the whiff of people passing. This *Furrière* for instance is for the rich women who arrive in taxis. I know this though I've never seen them. They're elderly and smell of my *Bonnemaman*—exotic cigarettes and a perfume that frightened me when I was little. It's the musk of the fox that's draped around the mannequin's neck and bears no price. Gleaming minks hug priceless shoulders but now a faceless, headscarfed woman hurries past me, coughing in the damp, twilight air.

All Hallows

As soon as they're out of the door me and my twin swap the sombre masks for clown-faces, scrubbing the ancient kitchen in a maelstrom of soap-bubbles and water-fights, chasing and shrieking through the apartment, dunking our heads in buckets. Meals are makeshift and fleet-of-hoof. Bedtimes are banished until we're through with baking and dancing. Well after midnight, when our cousins are sound asleep, we light the jack-o'-lanterns to show lost children the way home. We open the *Ordinaire* and a thousand djinns fly out. And before we can shout *Arrêtez!* they're cutting our long hair short with nail-scissors. And before it has time to grow again Tante Annie steps through the door, Oncle René turns purple and the demons hoot with mirth.

L'Heure du Déjeuner

Come rain and shine and upturned collars we seek one another's eyes as we scurry across Place Victor Hugo as if to some important business assignation or an eagerly anticipated rendezvous with a lover, or to a casual meeting with one of many friends. As we pass the brasserie we glance furtively into the glass-covered *terrasse* where groups of men and women are talking, drinking good wine and laughing as they slither oysters down their throats. A few sit alone at ease with themselves, reading *Le Monde* or *Le Figaro*, holding the espresso between index finger and thumb, the raised little finger chirpy in its signet ring. When we find each other out—which we always do—there's no feeling of shame, only of recognition as we hold each other's gaze and pass invisibly by.

Shadows

The hand striking the match is massive on the wall. The body extends up the sloping ceiling, its head above me. In my throat, sweet black coffee and the rasp of Disque Bleu. Someone's at the water-tap outside my locked door. There's a man coughing in the toilet where once a week I spend interminable night-hours squatting—arms outstretched to the walls on either side, thighs aching, guts racked following an evening of eating and drinking at an American doctor's apartment on Avenue Kléber, where the Scottish girl I met in class nannies three unhappy children. The body bending and stretching on the wall is my companion. Together we dance in the silence and bitter cold. I like the way her body speaks without making a sound. I like the way she moves, arching her arms, bowing her legs, spinning in a mock pirouette. Sometimes she does handstands, flipping over into a crab and sidling across the floor like Gregor Samsa. Now she's trembling with the cold. She pulls on layers of clothes: football-socks and jumpers and climbs into the low iron-bed. On the table, next to the candles, Balzac's *Le Père Goriot* and *The Great Hunger* by Cecil Woodham-Smith. Huge on the wall beside her, her friend takes a letter out of its envelope and begins to read.

The Marseillaise

Oh God is that Babu with his clothes snarled up in the dustcart, his face contorted as passers-by freeze to the spot or dart about gesticulating and shouting? The train draws in and I hurl myself onto the platform, down the stairway and into the street where I lurch blinking in the sunlight envisaging his eyes screwed up in agony. Or is it a dream? All around it's a perfect picture of spring as a band strikes up the *Marseillaise* and Erik Satie in fancy dress is reasoning like a blockhead: *The brain sees nothing, hears nothing of all that is happening around it, isolated as it is from the rest of the world.*

Clochard

He's here again, his body like a winter lizard clinging to the grille over the métro vent, resting his limbs in the steady draught of warm air. The *gendarme* disapproves, shakes him up and peels him from the pavement. My tutors say I should choose Maupassant or Baudelaire or Mallarmé. Eyebrows are raised when I say I want the living, the here and now. Why pick *Les Fleurs du mal*, I ask, when *le clochard* is my daily staple? I find him stacked up in the archives, row upon row, layer on layer, like a slice of the paupers' graves.

The Concierge's Cat

As I walk faster so do the steel-capped shoes going click click click along the empty lamp-lit street. I don't look round. I know it's the man on the métro who looks uncannily like Vincent van Gogh—he made my skin prickle with his pale unblinking eyes. How indignant I'd been with Rilke and yet he never spoke a truer word: I *am* unnerved and do *not* wish this man to sit near me. (Don't misunderstand, I hope I would embrace the leper.) This man's expression is no more detached from his soul than Vincent's. I can decipher his face and shoes—these shiny steel-tipped soles that clip maliciously behind me. I reach 59, press the release-button and push the heavy door. And as I fight to detach his hands I catch the panic in the cat's marmalade eyes before she turns and flees into the courtyard.

2. Storms & Stations

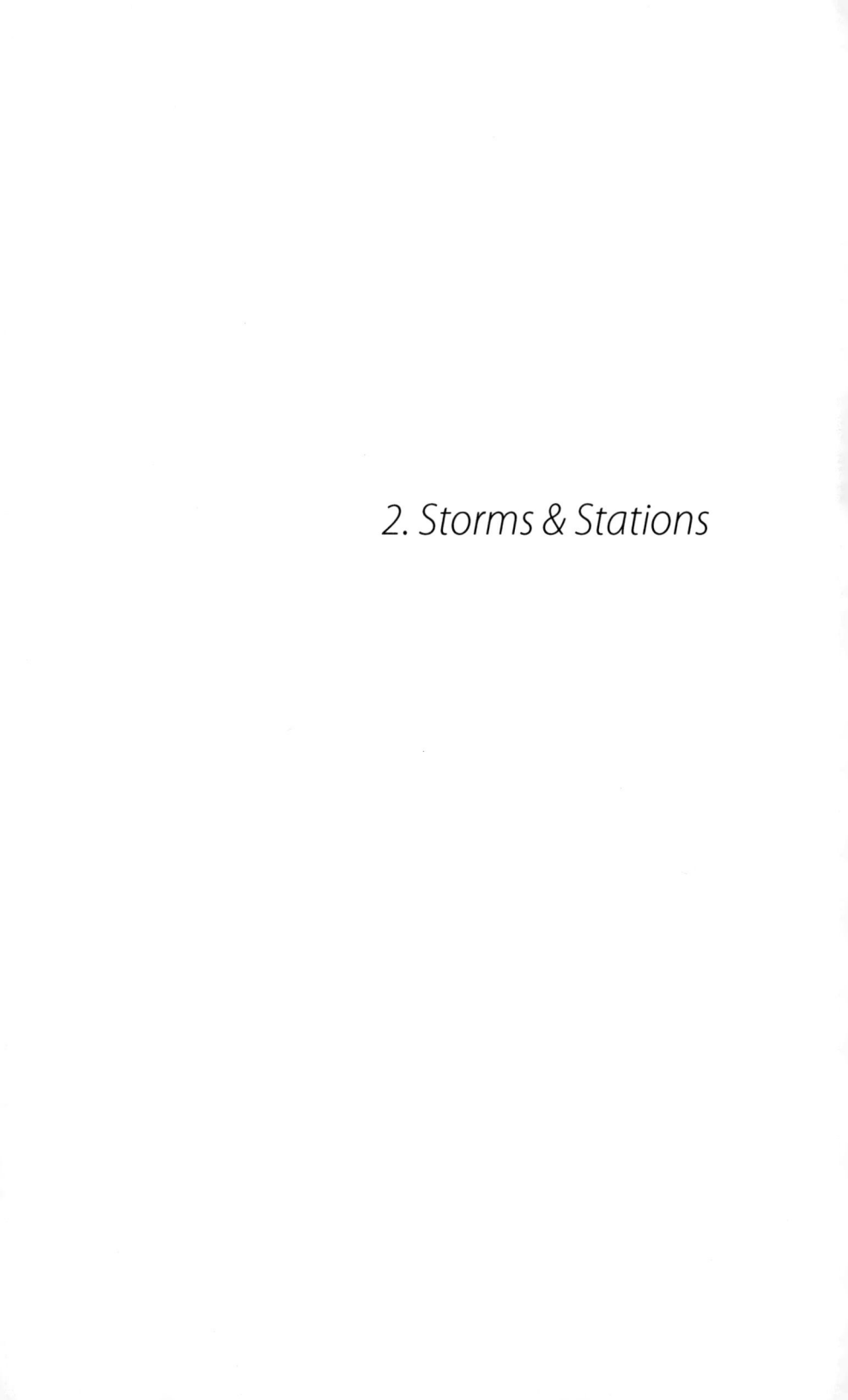

Montparnasse—Rambouillet

In all four seasons I have observed the stations—twelve of the sixteen stops to Rambouillet. I know them like the freckles on my skin, each with its own distinction. Now country folk are returning home from the Paris markets, motley collections of chickens and rabbits swinging from their arms in battered wicker baskets. I climb the high wooden steps into the gaping doors and greet the other passengers: a middle-aged couple, she cradling a giant turkey (*Deux dindes truffées, Garrigou?— Oui, mon révérend, deux dindes magnifiques bourées de truffes..*) and a fresh-faced soldier, kit-bag at his feet. The final six stops are music to my ears: Viroflay, Versailles-Chantiers, Saint-Cyr (the soldier gets out), Saint-Quentin-en-Yvelines, Trappes, La Verrière. I stare out of the window envisaging his face. When he sees me the whole of France lights up.

His Letters Are in Pencil

Addressed to Aylsham, Norfolk:— (olive-brown / HRH Elizabeth II Machin stamp) 10 a.m. Newhaven, Sussex: *I watched a big fat moon struggle out of the clouds tonight.*

Addressed to Sheringham, Norfolk:— (red-white-blue / Marianne) Sender:— c/o J. Walter Thompson, 17 Avenue Matignon, Paris: *I have been thinking of you ... glimpses of Bushey Place, barley fields and the tides at Blakeney.*

Addressed to Sheringham / forwarded to Bristol:— (blue-green / Émile Zola) Lévis St. Nom Girouard, 78 Yvelines: *Do all you can to come to Paris ... I want terribly to have you with me.*

Addressed to Bristol / forwarded to Sheringham:— (violet / Musiciens en Ivoire) Champs-Elysées: *... especially at night with poplars on the moon-lit horizon.*

Addressed to Sheringham / forwarded to 59 Rue Boissière, Paris 16e:— (green / Facteur: Journée du Timbre): *I shall have the ground floor of a small house in a beautiful village with country all around.*

The Light-Bearer

At last we escape the bar's crashing waves and clashing currents. Shaken, we sail round The Point where grey seals laze on the sand indifferent to the brush with death they witnessed—they've seen friends drown before. My brother's at the helm and H has the mainsheet. I'm clinging to the jibsheet, hands locked with cold, fingers burning from friction of the rope. In the safety of the Pit the tide is turning fast. We're not going to make it before the sea sucks out, leaving us stranded on the mudflats.

My brother and H are hauling the boat through the shallow water to the creek. They leave me slithering across the flats, mud oozing between my frozen toes. At last I reach the saltmashes, jumping over ditches and scrambling across a profusion of pools and little creeks, my feet and ankles glittering strangely.

The twilight's eerie, though the landmarks are familiar—buoys and moorings, rickety wooden bridges, Wiveton church silhouetted on the moon-lit horizon. Gulls and terns toss like celestial flotsam and a curlew cries out plaintively. Suddenly I see a figure making his way in my direction. He waves and we both start running, and I'm laughing as the man I love runs towards me, splashing through aster and samphire, fizzing with phosphorus like a human sparkler.

Tornado

The Canadian arrives like a tornado into our lives and into the soft changing colours of the valley's trees—the Lombardy poplars, the aspens with their shivering leaves where all the long summer we've given our selves to each other in the fields of Yvelines—driving slowly, feeding the ancient Volvo from bottles as it sputters along the hot, dusty roads. And into our evenings of reading out loud—*Lettres de mon Moulin* and *Illuminations*—he crashes in with *Leaves of Grass* and *Mountains and Rivers Without End*.

Crazy Horse

Life without women in the logging camps, life without men, serving time in the fire-lookout's cabin. Weekends we lie at his feet with our wine and rapt. Work-days you take the train into Paris. When you return he's cooking, telling stories of Little Bighorn, Crazy Horse and George Armstrong Custer. Oh he's good at tales and stories—has a theory on the scheme of things and individual freedom. But when it comes to mine he doesn't take kindly to a last-minute change of heart. And now, as you're kissing my bruised face and swollen lip, he's quoting Sitting Bull: *Each man is good in the sight of the Great Spirit.*

What Men Did Not Read in Their Hearts

I recoil with a terrible cold sensation in my heart. (Bastide)

She has enough consciousness to know she has a sharp conscience *the natural law is written and engraved in the soul.* The terrible fact is that for a few moments she allowed herself to be distracted and in those few moments she lost her conscience. It is fair to say she did not lose it entirely *it is human reason ordaining her to do good* so when, after a few minutes of blunted conscience, she snatched it back, the damage was done. Not sexual—she doesn't count the face and lip. It is her damaged conscience telling her *this command of human reason* it is damaged. It is this injury *the voice and interpreter of a higher reason* causing her such pain. That she changed her mind at the last instant does not set her free *our freedom must be submitted*. What difference does it make? She knows her conscience is a crueller witness than the creed she long ago dismissed.

Dark Matters

The aisle rocks with bodies clinging to leather straps. I wipe the steamed-up window and gaze down at the glow of a *remorqueur* moving slowly downriver through mist. Someone flicks a Gauloise to the floor and stubs it with his foot … all eyes switch to where it smoulders between two slats. I watch the barge disappear as if it's taking my life away. And yet … am I not merely *unaware* of the regions that are beyond us? Rilke says that the Arabs knew how to see the invisible and, if I had the right eyes, wouldn't I too perceive *how much greater are the black sectors*?

Landmarks & Boundaries

Soon I am outside the city, beyond the formality of Versailles and the strictures of St. Cyr. I have passed Trappes and am heading out into open countryside where my journey becomes easier through fields and sleeping villages. A dog barks. Owls gaze down from the branches of darkly-silhouetted trees. I sense their watchful presence. On and on I travel, taking long strides across valleys, streams, fallen trees. Nothing can stop me until at last the village comes into view. The Square is deserted, the petrol-sign swinging stiffly in the wind. The house is changed but it is the house and I know he is inside.

A golden light radiates under the door. Utter silence as I turn the knob. Gradually my eyes adjust. The room is electric with static and feathers that glide and spiral like a blizzard of snow-flakes. Then I see their bodies. The bed is a trampoline as they bounce entwined, their god-like beauty brushed by a ballet of swans.

I shut the door softly and leave for ever. My return to the city is difficult and confused for all the landmarks have changed. I stray into alien territory where the earth is scorched a deep terracotta-red and the isolation is primordial. Should I go forward or back? I retrace my steps, a stranger to myself. At last, stopping to rest and get my bearings, I notice an owl perched on a fence-post and tentatively ask him how long and far my journey will take me. With a detached expression he considers, blinking and ruffling a feather. I understand his reply. It is nothing less than I expected.

3. Apparitions & Intimations

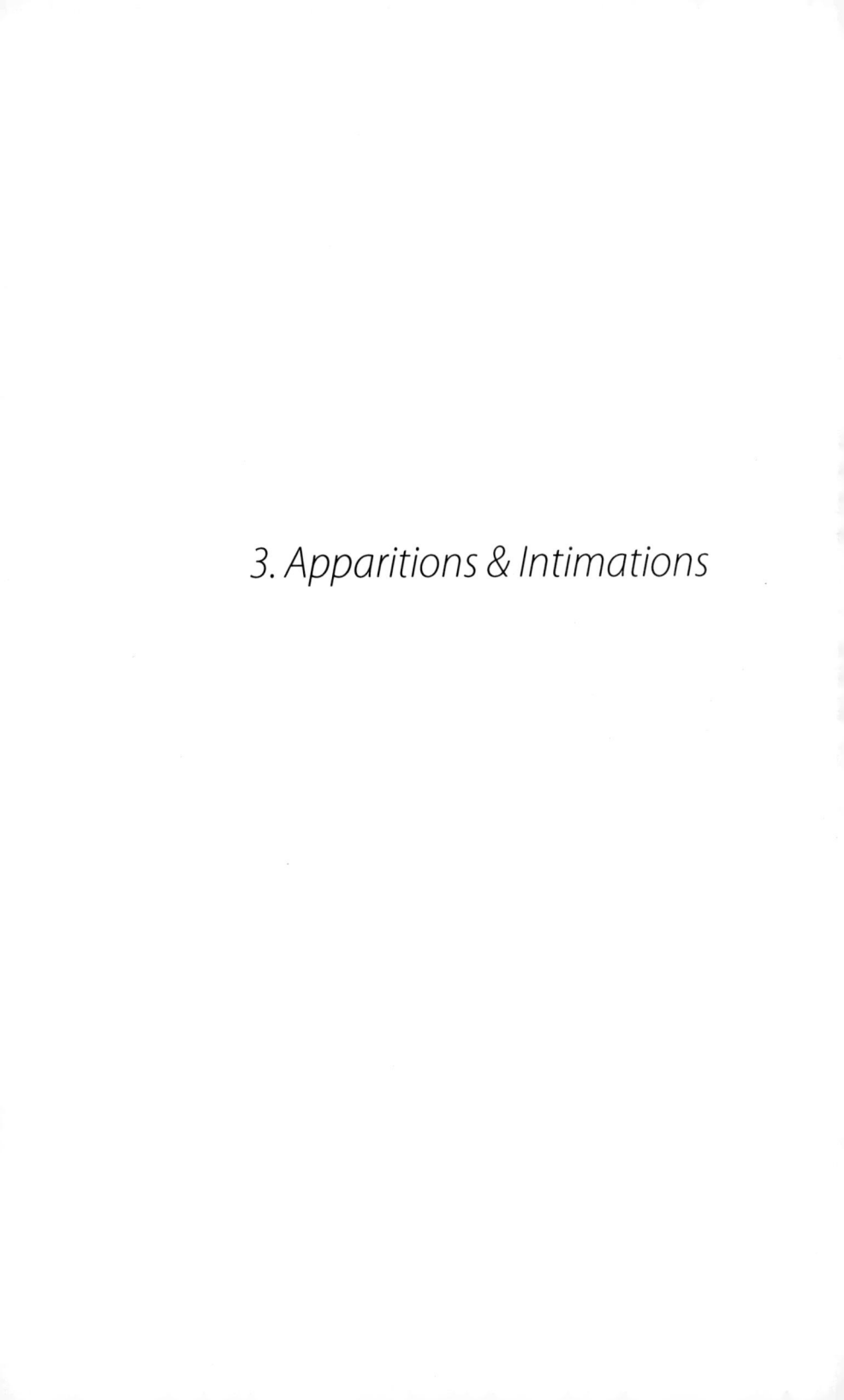

Algae Beds, Wyoming

Sometimes I wake up crying. My face is wet and everyone's asleep on seats around me. The driver, who's watching in his mirror, gesticulates and waves his pack of cigarettes. We smoke outside in silence as the shadows dance and the road hums and glows in the bus lights. The following day I thank him as he drops me off at the Hotsprings. I saw my twin being gun-whipped and gang-raped. Now I find her lying in the algae beds. Her eyes are emerald green and her hair's tangled blue—it oscillates in steam.

Now my dreams take me somewhere below the surface of water, which was already deeper than the grind of city pavements. Now they seem to take me inside the impact of violence, as if it's no longer enough to connect a dead body with the elements and vegetation. I'm searching through rubber, leather and metal for any trace of her. But already they're clearing the road and I'm getting frantic. I want her head, her face. Fate gives me an indistinct remnant of leg clinging to steel, so I stare in a last ditch effort. At last it disengages, turns to face me.

After this it is easier to understand my lover. I'd thought he was fooling, going around with a sheet over his head. I reached up to kiss him and realised that the sheet was to disguise the fact that he had no head. Oh no, I thought, this cannot be: a man with no head cannot be alive, and I panicked ever so slightly to think I'd kissed the wrong man. So I pulled off the sheet to find a neck where the head should be, and I didn't know who it was until it opened its eye.

Disturbances

Marina says that a wind blows over desert sand chiselling stripes, ridges or wavy lines the way that chemicals move like fluids through tissue, fixing genetic patterns. She mentions the stripes on zebras & tigers, the spots on hyenas & leopards. And now, as twilight soaks into mountains, she tells me about the big brown blotches on her body, how each long vacation she returns to the kibbutz where the hot sun erases them for a year, and wonders if broken symmetries are like promises, contracts or legacies betrayed?

On the Greyhound

My companions have transmogrified into monkeys and apes. I can tell by his gait, knuckle-walking, that Kurtz is a chimp and Karen, who moves on the flats of her fingers, a baboon. My only comfort is the old dictum: *manners makyth man*. I am still susceptible to human taboos because *I* am still *me*. But when our driver, who's warned he'll tolerate no smoking of dope or even cigarettes in prohibition Utah, lopes up the gangway as a massive quadruped, my life flashes in front of me. The bus erupts. Howlers set up a terrible racket. The civilities that have distinguished me vanish. I try to smash the window but oh gesticulating image! A gibbering rhesus monkey mimics me!

On the Highway

The mule deer still have velvet on their antlers as they perch on cliffs and roam in pine forests through rough, steep canyons to the open grasslands, feeding at dawn and dusk. Here the sage and blue grouse nest before bedding in shrubby brush land. The man from THE DEER AND FISHING COMMISSION says that during fall they try to cross the highway to reach more hospitable ridges, but since the sixty human fatalities the deer are now fenced in, dying from cold and starvation.

He gestures towards the Greyhound's open windows, sweeping his arm in a wide arc. All this land is to be commercialised for coal-mining, oil refineries and jade factories. I gaze out at the vast terrain. *Ten million years ago an ocean floor glides like a snake beneath the continent, crunching up the old seabed until it's as high as alps.* Thousands of miles away, a mother blackbird broods her five eggs in the scrub outside my bedsit, while a buff-tailed bumble bee shelters from an equinoctial downpour, the tiny baskets on her hind-legs brimming with yellow pollen.

The Christian Hostel for Men and Women

Deep in Mormon country, it's the only place that welcomes me and my friends at 3 a.m.: the Professor and Jester into a chalet and Marina and me through eerie streets to the luxury of a bed. Three days ago we asked ourselves how often the wheel of fortune spins you a ready-made buddy: someone who's a twin like you and to your English/French is German/Israeli. Stripping to our pants I see the dark brown blotches on her body. Too tired for sleep we lie on the bed drinking from cans and find a pamphlet on a shelf above our heads: *The Girl Who Loved Nazis*. We read out loud drinking our beer as the story unfolds of a girl whose need to conform makes her "deaf to Jesus". And just before dawn, Marina tells me how hard it is—this disease passed on in the genes.

Warnings

I

Richard Cooley: Spends his weekends fishing & hunting and every fortnight polishes & waxes his sixty-four-foot emerald truck with its glittering silver chimneys. Garden products—celery, grapes, melons, nectarines. Hates strawberries—they bruise so easily he's forced to drive slowly. LITTLE SNAKE RIVER flashes in the headlamps as we roar up the mountain. Loves women, longs for a woman of his own to come home to. Thunder crashes & lightning forks across the roiling Colorado sky. Warns us not to judge all truck drivers by himself: 25% are bad. There's a stretch of highway where men drive their women to pose as hitch-hikers as they hide in their cars in the brush. When a trucker stops they jump out, beat him up and rob him. Lives in Arkansas near Stamps. Does he know why the caged bird sings? Pays for our room & food. Is small & swarthy & good.

II

As the mileometer/odometer ticks off the distance to Grand Canyon my body begins to shiver. A Ouija is inside me scribbling under my skin, yelling in loud capital letters not to go. But Richard Cooley refuses to drop me off in Death Valley. I wouldn't mind: my mind doesn't shy from the skeletons of cattle. My ideomotor instinct knows I am animal too. A threat more devastating emanates from the auras of Grand Canyon. My teeth chatter as my skin erupts in goose-bumps. What malevolence seeps out of seventeen million years to single me out? I don't even want to look. I take a picture of Marina and book on the next bus out. But the time-zone scrambles my watch. I forget to change my body-clock and see the Greyhound disappear en route to Phoenix, Houston, New Orleans.

Old Man

Who is this old man who comes to me in dream—long legs and solitude stretched before him like poverty? Where does he come from to show me his despair, and to make me feel I'd sooner die than leave him? Why does he persist in showing me the same things life reveals if not to insist that there's no difference between this love for a stranger and that for my twin the time it seemed our driver would reverse over the cliff? Sitting in front, I could easily get out and save myself, leaving my twin and her child to perish in the back. But the thought of remaining weighed more than the act of escaping and tipped the balance.

Even the men, women and children I've had to leave stay with me like flash-backs—the "destined" accidents of life. The man slumped on the métro steps, clutching a board with the words *vétéran de guerre: veuillez aider* crawling like roaches over sores exposed through filthy gauze. The woman who attacked me, beating my head and scratching, leaving her skin on my skin, her blood on my blood, her eyes, her screams, her smudged lipstick forever living in me. And those lovers by the Seine: the mole on her leg and he big and nuzzling like a badger into the neck of her coat, oblivious to the child's rusty spade and the man's abandoned boot.

The toddler on Midsummer Common in bright yellow oilskins, splashing in the rain and puddles, paddling up to us on little bandit legs as if in a surfeit of happiness. In the pub, Puffing Billy, Friar Tuck, and Nick the Schiz who showed me his paintings, said he'd wanted to be a sculptor but they wouldn't let him loose with the blades. In Addenbrookes, the two boys aged five and fourteen, breathing and warm to my touch, both donating their organs, machine-alive, neither living nor dead.

Aegean Sea

Disappointing is the black volcanic sand. Disappointing the uninvigorating sea. Each day, as the sun climbs to its zenith in the blue sky, D takes my hand and we stroll around the harbour, admiring the colourful fishing boats and the racks of nets and octopus hanging out to dry, greeting the old men who sit in the shade mending their nets. We linger at quayside taverns and I gaze at the sparkling sea, longing to fling myself in and to swim out to the mermaids' rocks. Every day I imagine it. Every day it fails to satisfy and I emerge with a malaise that feels both physical and psychological, for a flame hath stolen beneath my skin.

We talk about K every day and times it seems to me I'm not far off dying. But who knows what truth is? Was her resolve to leave us and go to Lesbos on her own more evasive than my decision to write the verse she's reading as if it were my own? As for us, we read, make love, sleep, and go out to buy peaches, returning hours later to remove the invisible spines of prickly pears from our bodies. We've made friends with locals who are teaching us the alphabet and how to ask directions—Πού είναι ο φούρνος; Evenings, everyone's on the streets and in the morning the face of Papadopoulos stares out from newspapers.

A few dusty streets from the harbour, the orange cement-mixer sits on the white balcony like a theatre set or an Edward Hopper. The landlady's little daughter plays while her dad sleeps off the nightshift. Lodgers come and go. The airless nights are frequently disturbed by the sound of creaking bedsprings as drops of sweat run down my trembling body. One dawn a terrible commotion penetrates my fug of retsina and ouzo. Returning from his shift, the landlady's man walks under the balcony the instant it collapses.

Cortège

Even from this distance I know she is sunburnt and peeling, the tender skin in pink salty patches on the tip of her nose and cheekbones. The queues of travellers waiting for airplanes are sucked from my consciousness like a movie spooling in reverse. The shouts and occasional cries fade out like the procession this morning when we stood aside as the cortège passed slowly, the women beating their breasts and wailing, our landlady and her child leading the coffin-bearers. When K sees us she stuffs her book in a side-pocket and heaves her rucksack onto her shoulders. I wait my turn to kiss her, to inhale the Aegean wind with its whiff of ancient mule paths, olive groves and white boulders. She's elusive with distance and time and I want to take in my two hands *the head that I shall dream of and 'twill not dream of me.*

4. Nightmares & Daymares

Nigg Bay, Aberdeen

The air is sweet with hyacinths along Claremont Street and Great Western Road and I'm eager to get out of town to the docks and further round the coast to Nigg Bay where on stormy nights the sea crashes over the rocks and the foghorn breaks into my nightmares. This is where I cycle on my afternoons off to read my library books and to shake out my thoughts in the bracing salty air. The problem of Katúsha Máslova is occupying my mind. I'm absorbed by her pretty face surrounded by dark ringlets, her black eyes sparkling with the strange squint that bewitches Nekhlúdov, his confused feelings of pity and revulsion when he visits her in prison. I feel great sympathy for his sin against her, for I have left my own in the outskirts of Paris. Unable to bear the weight of my action or to piece together the smithereens of my heart, I arrived in Aberdeen with nothing but a small suitcase and 200 duty-frees. And it was right here walking along Market Street that I suddenly knew I would suffer for many years to come.

Nazareth House

A careless gesture and a girl is running through smoke-filled corridors, down never-ending stairs, voices, shouts and screams filling her ears: *You're the witch of the place! The wicked witch!* Where's mama to care for her, tend her burns? Where's mama who left her here, small girl among enemies?

No rich father for her. No wealthy brewer to spoil her, leave her all his money. No lover to woo her, ask her hand in marriage. Doomed to this place she's a cross between a waxwork and a skeleton with sad moving eyes. She didn't do it. Wasn't her who dropped the cigarette.

She's a middle-aged woman now, lives here and earns her keep. Someone's mistake cost her her freedom and she will never bring herself to say: *Take the pencil and write under my name, "I forgive you"*.

Sleep

Night breathes, walls creak and within dark rooms the unspeakable happens. I try to stay awake. Nightmares pursue me with malevolent eyes and crazed faces. Only the foghorn breaks the silence. Each morning I try to open my eyes, touch them and wince. I grope along the corridor clutching the wall-tiles. This is the dawn ritual of bathing and soaping: opening my eyes to the daymares.

Loons & Quines

At Jamieson's Quay loons and quines are running about or squatting in little groups rolling their tallymashers. I smile back at their inquisitive grubby faces, no longer shocked by the sight of them playing barefoot on the cobbles. Nekhlúdov is deeply disturbed by the children's suffering. For how long, he wonders, can they remain innocent surrounded by brutality and neglect—the baby with its scrawny twisted neck, its tiny ashen face contorted into the grimace of an old man? Nigg Bay glitters in the sun, the cobalt sea broken up by dancing horses. I sit next to the foghorn gazing out and thinking of the children at breakfast. Frankie with the beautiful face and graceful bearing, his father locked up in Glasgow Prison. Where are the mothers of these fifteen boys standing behind their chairs? Who is listening to their mute pleas? Who will hear them silently begging to be summoned by the wicked nun for bacon, mealies and a piece?

Not Jenever/Not Friend

Not thinking of gin's inventor: the physician Franciscus Sylvius. Not considering juniper, anise, caraway or coriander. (Thinking: Dutch courage.) Nor citrus botanicals such as lemon & bitter orange-peel. (Thinking: friends do not let you down.) Nor angelica root & seed (friends do not abandon you penniless) orris & licorice root (compelling you to hitch a lift in a gin-smuggling truck en route to Birmingham). Not cinnamon, cubeb, lime & grapefruit-peel. (Friend not friend.) Not dragon eye, saffron, baobab, frankincense, nutmeg or cassia bark. (Notfriend not ask how you eventually get to college.) No thought for kidney & stomach ailments. (Notfriend not think how a man can lose control. How his eyes turn manic and his strength makes yours a matter of life/not life.) No thought of lumbago, gallstones or gout.

Absurd Nights

With fantastic ease my daytime room transforms at night, assumes proportions of a universe. I hear other students breathe as their dreams swirl past the window. Their vital bodies surround me like stars I cannot reach and I think of him in Paris. I read obsessively. I find that the more absurd friends are the more sympathetic and authentic. The doctor prescribes medication, tells me to break my affair with Ionesco. I become excessively gregarious, running around with drinks and biscuits. In the morning my head is better but my limbs have a will of their own.

5. Rooms & Roads

Tempelhof

In our parents' house my twin's dressing-gown hangs empty on the bedroom door. She's died many times before. Choking on a boiled sweet. Flailing in the deep-end till a giant plucks her to safety. I save her from ten year-old Grix Smith, swinging him to the ground, trembling at the awed applause. Worst of all is her recurring disappearance at the Mill Pond. I watch powerless as she struggles in the whirlpool's currents, as her angel-face vanishes through the sluice gate. But now the Principal's trying to defeat me. I must sort out my eating and sleeping. My grades will suffer seismic disruption. How can I explain that she's dead until I see her, live where she lives? As the plane touches down my body-clock shifts.

A Road in Berlin

On my daily route to or from Oranienstrasse via the Penny Supermarkt for a bottle of cheap dry white to drive *The force that through the green fuse*. A road equidistant from the Kurfürstendamm of my once-a-week treat at the Ice Cream Parlour and the Kurfürstendamm of the glamorous prostitutes. The road with the *Ringbahn* train screeching along the elevated tracks, sparks flying; with the Turkish *Gastarbeiter*, with all the little ateliers and artisan shops: the cobblers and picture-framers, the sewing-machines and joinery. Everywhere movement. Old men struggling with ladders and planks of wood; young men balancing massive panes of glass; little trucks bouncing over cobblestones; bicycles, tricycles and mopeds; the heady smells of paint, rubber tyres and sawdust; the pervasive whir and whine of sewing-machines, of lathes shaping and scraping and moulding in a symphony of industry. This is the road with the mad women where at any time of day you see them hanging out of third-floor windows, screaming and gesticulating. The artisans ignore them. If they glance up, they look down again. I never see them laugh or make a "knowing" gesture. Yes, this is the road where lost women pop out of windows like cuckoos from the clocks of ancient minutes.

Der Rote Stern Verlag

Her stomach is large, her legs & arms like spindles. I find her behind the book-stacks crying. I ask what it is (breaks my heart to see my twin like this) but can't hear a word above the machines. She wipes her eyes and we return to the endless collating. She's two months to go. He's at the machines covered in grease & ink. She loves him and longs for the child. We pack & stack: *Mao Tse-tung und Marximus-Leninismus*. On the buses women point and whisper—she looks like a pregnant child. She's an expert one-ring/one-pan conjurer: *Kartoffelpuffer; Boulette mit Kohlrabi; Bockwurst mit Linsen*. She calls all toys and baby-clothes "divine" or "little angels". I lend her my set-text: *Mutter Courage und Ihre Kinder*.

A Room in Northfield

I try to like the girl who shares my room. I pick out all the positive things like "twin", "Irish", "can be funny", but still I cannot like her. She's most dangerous when intimate. She wants to make me her *confidante* but I know it's ammunition. Through her white nightie I see the dark current. As she sleeps in the bed next to mine my hair stands on end. Such a storm raged through her that night at college. The Principal called the police and they called me. She was laid out on a table thrashing and incoherent. The police asked if I'd be alright. No, I'm not alright and I hide my protection under my pillow.

Reservoir

I did not know her but the girl haunts me. Night after night I follow her in my mind—like me she is someone's daughter. She makes her way through dimly-lit streets to the black water, muttering, pleading, drinking red wine that trickles down her chin, onto her dress. She thinks of his sweet-talking, his verse recitals. She stares at the waning moon: now she is no one's muse. The sky lowers and the trees begin to whisper. She fills her pockets. The water attracts her with the power of his rejection.

On a Cliff at Hayle

For Anne

She transforms my life, makes me believe, restores me. We share a room in a big sunny house. Eat smarties for breakfast and cakes for dinner. Practise teaching at the Girls' Grammar. Run for the buses—Moseley to Shirley—envying the Woolworth's girls. Share heart-breaks and love stories. Play Nielson endlessly. Argue politics, philosophy and religion. Hitch-hike from the unfinished M5 to the Scilly Isles via Bristol. Wash our hair on the ferry drinking Whisky Mac. Sleep either side of a man, in his triple sleeping-bag. Now, perched on a cliff at Hayle, watching the sun melt into St. Ives Bay, she predicts our futures will be different. I foretell the life-long thread between us.

Litany

i.m. Marie Dooley (1960–1989)

I guess, after all, the old men had a point about Leonard Cohen. But she loves him, plays him over and over: *Tonight will be Fine, Birds on a Wire, Sisters of Mercy*. And I don't imagine he replaces the cab-drivers any more than Jesus does, but between them they are giving her a sense of peace she hasn't found in years. In fact she might say she's making *her* peace, setting *her* scene. She moves between the traditional—*O Mary, full of grace, pray for us*—and the improvised—*I have tried in my way to be free*—as between two altars: calmer, increasingly serene, lighting the candles, uniting the sounds and lyrics in a new personal litany without conflict or contradiction. She buys October flowers, carries them to the church and leaves them with her lit candles. She gives away a whole white bunch to a man with a dog.

The MAFF, Whitehall

His eyes are deep brown pools of fathomless wisdom and patience, like the perception reflected in Sylvia's owls she occasionally glimpses in the eyes of Casmilus, her "dear one", which she calls his "old-fashioned" look. Abdul doesn't resemble Casmilus. He is small with thick black hair and a moustache peppered with Camel cigarette-ash. Together we have set up a resistance to the repugnant Tony. Tony is to Abdul what Clem is to his poor brother Tiny: malicious, pursuing only to persecute and sneer. I am keeping a journal, though not on yellow paper. Does he know that the doctor is a world authority on sphagnum?

We pore over Abdul's book and I promise to scour the Scottish bogs and bring back samples. Thirty-four species and he shows me pictures of the rare Olive bog-moss and Baltic bog-moss. And because I'm going to St. Abb's Bay he illustrates flushes that occur at sea-level on the damp shell sand: Short-Tooth hump-moss and the liverworts Irish ruffwort and the rare Gilman's notchwort.

Abdul is not like Tiny but is he likewise crushed in love? He lives alone, this erudite man, who wears corduroy trousers and a lambswool jumper in the hot July lunchtime. Was/is there a "dear one" in his life—a Vera Hennessey met sailing on the Bosphorus with a Turkish mama? Not wishing to pry I ask him how to transport sphagnum from Scottish mires to Charing Cross. He's not listening. With a distant look in his eyes he's reciting: *Each species has its own texture and distinctive hue: deep red through orange and ochre to delicate browns and greens.*

Christian Street, Whitechapel

For Sister Mary Teresita Heenan

The school was the first to have a Jewish headteacher. The girls don't know. Nor do they stroke thirty milking cows on Goodman's Fields. Nor see the West End. They only watch Dick Turpin hide Black Bess in the Red Lion after the shoot-out. Only see with their own wide-eyes *Great numbers of loose, idle and disorderly Persons, as Street-Robbers and Common Night-Walkers, so to infest the streets, that it will be very dangerous for His Majesty's subjects to pass the same.*

Like me they hear & fear the Headmistress's rosary & habit. We shiver in the snow where she makes me take the register to chill this passion for love stories. By contrast the Deputy does not make the stick her habit. Her face is open and her rosary sings. As she enters the classroom she hears a pin drop: *I will notice neither the golden sunset, nor the distant sails descending towards Harfleur, and when I arrive, I will place on your grave a bunch of green holly and flowering heather.* When I leave, she gifts me her own small collection.

Flight

I'm walking drunkenly home through the after-hour streets. I do not wish to go home. I do not wish to return to a woman I used to love. A woman whose fits of rage and jealousy reduce me to jelly. And because I cannot fight my only recourse is flight. Anaïs Nin says art is a journey of personal growth and development—as if life isn't? I dislike her tone when she says it's a pity Sylvia Plath is revered by the young as a cult figure: her poetry did not allow her to transcend herself: her despair became for an instant stronger than her love. Tomorrow's the day. Everything stays except me. Books, clothes, records and my favourite poster of a figure on top of a cliff, gazing across a winding path to the beach and out to sea.

6. Death & Magic

The World Is a Swaying Lantern

The world is a swaying lantern and I am a spirit lost in the urban wilderness. A muffled bus glides by, the lucky ones inside lit-up like spectres staring through peep-holes in the whited-out windows. Cars have been abandoned. Road markings and boundaries have vanished. I have relinquished my bed, dreams and reading but cannot get to teach. If only a droshky or troika would enter the scene! There are no announcements at the station. All is still, silent, gagged. Who is the figure edging beside the train tapping the undercarriage with a metal pole, the bell-sound ringing out in the petrified silence? Who is the cloaked woman pacing the platform near the engine, trembling and distraught?

Theories on the Origin of a Name

i) The Officer of the town is commonly known as Portreve—a word anciently founded in Portgereve = limit, bound or precinct of the rule or office. Ham = homestead, village or town. Grevesham/Gravesham: home of the town's Officer.

ii) Grave from Greva used in the Doomsday Book 1086. Belonging to Odo, Bishop of Bayeux and called "Gravesham", probably derived from "graaf-ham": the home of the Reeve/Bailiff of the Lord of the Manor.

iii) From Greva/ Latin Grava = a coppice or small wood or grove. Gravesend: the end of the grove.

iv) Gravesend: denotes the town's waters as being the furthest point for burials at sea. During the Black Death the corpses of plague victims were brought here to avoid spreading the disease in London.

The Ferry

Swings out from the West Street Pier churning a wake at the stern and swirling eddies to starboard and port. Mr Peggotty, Ham and the Micawbers are sailing away to begin a new life in Australia. Pip's rowing Magwitch downriver from London in the hope of waylaying the steamer bound for Hamburg. A police patrol speeds upriver. It's seven minutes across to Tilbury on the bend of the river. Tugs are docking a Russian coal-carrier at the Power Station. My colleague does this twice a day. She teaches geography, rides a moped to and from the ferry. She has freckles, auburn hair and a smile like my sister's. Weekends she runs a hot-dog stand at Greys Thurrock.

A Whiff of the Medieval

Evenings after work I love to hang around by the pier and in this I'm not alone. Men stop to lean against the rail and roll a cigarette. We watch the watermen ushering huge container ships up the estuary, the smells wafting down-river from Bowater's paper mills. Now and then a group of Sikh women pass by, returning from the factories, chatting, calling out to a straggling child. There's something in the atmosphere that pulls me to the quaysides. The characters come alive—Pepys, for instance, though in 1667 it was not the tugboats but the Dutch: *we do plainly at this time hear the guns play.*

I bring my lover/s to The Three Daws and over pints of hoppy ale tell him stories of staircases and tunnels that helped sailors escape the press gangs, smugglers to ply their trade; about pilgrims crossing the river on their way to the Shrine of St. Thomas at Canterbury—I know he'll appreciate this whiff of the medieval. He likes The Miller's Cottage on Shrubbery Road, still grinding wheat in the nineteenth century. I observe him observing the paintings on the wall and think again of Pepys: *A good handsome wench I kissed, the first I have seen in a great while.*

I give my parents a wood-mounted print of *The Fight Between Carnival and Lent*. I think it will appeal to their respective temperaments. They say they like it but hang it in the spare-room and when I stay I gaze at it for hours. The Thames seeps into the atmosphere, steeping the town in an ancient wash. I bring him to The Kent where we sit among sailors and transvestites. Its no-nonsense friendliness attracts me. Like the resilience of the children in my class: Johnny with the glass eye, Danny with the hook hand.

Gordon Gardens

The music teacher lives in a flat near the Gurdwara in Clarence Place. As we stroll out for an ice-cream and to walk in Gordon Gardens she tells me that Rimsky-Korsakov wrote part of his First Symphony here. (I know *The Flight of the Bumble Bee* and a game called *Corsets Off*.) Chinese Gordon on the other hand cared for the town's "poor boys", providing food and clothes from his Army wage. She's fierce on rhythm, beat and time— keeps the kids to the track like clockwork soldiers.

The Chair

Flew through the window when I wasn't watching. The boy outside the door says it happened by magic or accident. Believing magic and knowing accident I extract a promise and the boy walks home to the Estate. In the Head's Office the Head, the Head of Year and the Head of Faculty speak sternly. You mean to say you *trust* him? they exclaim. I do not mention magic. Next morning the boy is prompt. The Head scratches his head.

Wodnesdaeg

Outside the pub blown by the wind the Hoodeners are ritual prancing under the winter moon. I follow their steps, leaps, above-the-head clapping as Dobbin goes snap snap snap and the Waggoner starts to sing *This old woman is our Molly, she looks rather melancholy.* The rope to clack the jaw passes through the back of the head but I don't see it. This is my childhood phantom of windy nights when *the trees were crying loud and ships were tossed at sea.* It's Der Schimmelreiter riding the dyke, a pair of burning eyes flaring from the horse's ghostly face. Or Invicta Rampant resisting William in 1066. Not for me the lower jaw gently accepting coins! Not for me *hooded hide hoaden.* This is Wōden who gave us Wednesday, bringing us death, magic, poetry, prophecy.

Gillingham to Gravesend

I

The line is as fine as a thread between life and death. The breath is held, tension suspended not to be palpable. Night helps, conceals a paling face and trembling hands as we drive, darkling woods either side of the road. The headlights blaze and a petrified hare fakes dead. The driver asks me questions and I read his mind, my own leaping ahead, aching, synapses flashing. He's tracing my earlier steps for witnesses of the clothes I'm wearing, my movements after missing Gravesend and hitching a lift. I mention the Gillingham police who offered me a cell—keep to myself the absurd craving for breakfast.

II

How cool and detached she is. She asks about his sports-gear in the back as he accepts her cigarette. How skilfully he steers in the dark, lassoing the dialogue back where he wants it. She's taut as a string, fine-tuned to the tiniest vibrations. He asks who's expecting her and a voice invents waiting parents, a call from a kiosk. As he sets her down at a house that is not where she lives, she implores a phantom mum or dad to open a curtain, come to the door. At last she stands in the deserted street. He makes a frantic grab through the window, burning her arms and wrists, ordering her down to the mist-clad river.

The Greasy Spoon

Through smudges in the steamed up window it's possible to imagine the occupants are permanent fixtures, chessmen/actors switching squares. The props are always the same: Formica tables bearing a Woolworth's cruet of salt and pepper, a bottle of malt vinegar, a red plastic tomato and a yellow one for mustard. Out-of-work men and women are hunched over steaming plates and I don't let on I'm bunking off. I drink my mug of Camp coffee huddled in my coat of many colours. But work is a blessing I cannot always feel. Stronger is the anonymity of sitting here in peace.

A Tale of Two (I)

She is my earliest memory. Bouncing opposite me in the twin pram. Reaching out to grab each other's hair. She arrives on her Kawasaki with Stefan on the back. I lift him off the bike and love him like he's mine. She shares my bed and he rides on the songs of *Melanie* as we finish the feast and wine. They pump the empty out of the flat. They fill the running-on-empty with fun and love and sad and when they leave the flat drains out.

A Tale of Two (II)

In a room full of crying smoke I await my lover/s. I smoke because I cannot betray them. Cry because I cannot give them up. They entered my life as two. I cannot choose. One at a time they arrive. If you assume I two-time you are mistaken. I do not indulge in subterfuge. Nor manipulate. I wait wait wait for one of them to call. Did I tell you they are brothers? Did I say that I save this restaurant for one, this pub for the other?

In a Street off Echo Square

Frost laces the window. The blizzard blows in behind me when the old woman opens the door. Her gnarled arthritic hands are shades of purple, the skin sacrament thin. I stare at the grate where a single lump of coal glows dimly. Did a dark-haired man knock on her door at the strike of midnight? Did she receive: salt for seasoning, silver for wealth, coal for warmth, a match for kindling and bread for sustenance?

7. Stalker

And the Sun Will Shine

A pair of eyes is skimming the surface of the hedge at the far end of the scrub my landlord calls a garden. They're staring right at me and they are not Feliciano's. Nor felicitous. Nor blind. Not Steinbeck's, Rilke's or Van Gogh's. They belong to the man walking the street behind the hedge. I cannot see the man, only the eyes that hold me like a magnet. My eyes cannot repel them. They attract him right up to the grubby window where I sit with my mouth locked open and my fork frozen in mid-air. The man's not looking at me. He's like a manic puppet jumping around the scrub, sizing up the three-floor house of empty bedsits as Feliciano sings the *Hitchcock Railway*.

Singing in the Rain

Normally a sanguine person, I'm sometimes given to argument. On this occasion it's with Steinbeck in the shower. My contention is his claim that *people rarely sing for joy*. Today, like most Saturday mornings, I'm preparing to take the train to meet Van Gogh at the National Gallery. He's promised to illuminate the brushstrokes around his self-watching eyes and I'm full of joy and sweet anticipation. I slap shampoo into my hair singing and laughing in Steinbeck's face. Is it not possible to sing sad songs from joy and cheerful songs from sorrow? I remind him of the method he's developed to describe beauty in an agitated mood and to invent terrible deeds from a peaceful disposition. He gives me an exasperated look and I resume singing until I notice a giant sunflower nodding behind the semi-opaque front door. I step out of the shower to check if it's Vincent. On my way to the station I sing to keep my spirits up. *Humans sing most beautifully in pain and longing.*

'Rose-bush' at My Window

The journal is written on the verso of a large notebook while on the recto fiction grows by fifteen hundred words per day. I'm reading the *journal* of the *novel* I've just read. I envisage the long-dead Nobel Prize-winner writing every morning: verso/recto/verso/recto. As the rose-bush taps my window (verso) I sooth my nerves by reading the book (recto). I read in bed and the author holds me. He loves women the way my lover/s love women, only he's more available. The intermittent tapping sets up a rhythm with the throbbing of my tooth. It fills the gap between the curtain's hem and the window's sill. The author draws me close and comforts me. He has two broken marriages and two small sons. He loves his sons and I love him for loving them. Sometimes he drinks too much and I love that too. The persistent tapping beats a tattoo on my tooth and infiltrates my brain.

Company

These days I party every evening. Wine courtesy of Monsieur le Patron and generous supplies of Winstons. It's not your regular type of party with music and dancing. In fact you might say it's somewhat singular. You'll think it's funny and I, too, laugh from time to time. At first I called it my reading party. I invited Rilke but he didn't empathise and I couldn't engage. Even Steinbeck lost his touch so I busied myself instead: my reading parties became sewing parties. It's cramped under the table but I can just squeeze in my batik skirt. I think it's the hem's endlessness that gives me the shakes. By half-past eight Monsieur and Winston are depleted and I'm trembling from head to toe. Before the clock-tower strikes nine I will hear the smash of my splintering window.

The Compulsion

To emerge from my hideout and stagger to the mirror. To face the stranger in my face. Who is she in the white of her face, like the white of Robert Wyman's *Twin*? Is it this white that fills the stalker's dreams and fuels his nightly propulsion to the one-way mirror? The reflection is distorted. If I break the mirror I'm done for.

Inside the Telephone Kiosk

I've decided to bring my Dictionary of Etymology. I start with *oxymoron*. No. I start by watching the two roads: The Overcliffe passes my bedroom window and St. James's Street gives access to my door. I never see anything suspicious from my sentry-box. I know I'm being watched and look up *paradox* (Gk. *paradoxos* "contrary to expectation"). Every now and then I step out to let someone make a call. The advantage of a reference book is that it doesn't attract attention. While *East of Eden* might aggravate, *Sonnets to Orpheus* would surely invite a smashed window and that's precisely why I'm here. *Serendipity*: coined by Horace Walpole … in a letter to Horace Mann … from the Persian fairy tale 'The Three Princes of Serendip', whose heroes were always making discoveries, by accidents and sagacity, of things they were not in quest of. Last week the police came. They examined the airgun pellets in the wall and boarded up the window and the door. I flick to **P** […]:from Gk. *psykhe* "mind" + *pathos* "suffering".

Panda

Noun 1. *patrol car, police car, prowl car, voiture pie, Streifenwagen, auto della polizia.*
So-called because of the black & white magpie panels? No. Due to the bear's blinkered vision & slow lethargic actions. I make a statement, fill in forms. They drive me home, shine torches into the scrub behind the hedge, tell me I'm not secure as shadows leap on the wall. They call me *love*. This isn't love I say. They say they'll catch him, just a question of… Whose time I say. They'll have a panda pass by. It's midnight I say.
Noun 2. *cat-foot black-and-white; assumed to be docile, has been known to attack.*

Signet Ring

Between the curtain's hem and the window's sill is a *Signet/Seal/Sign*. If I don't act the police will find my body with the crime pinned to it. Is intuition rational—these whisperings under the skin that break out in cold sweat? THE OXFORD MANUAL OF CLINICAL MEDICINE describes tumours with signet-ring morphology but not the physiognomic and physiological changes to my face and skin. *Signetum/Signum*. Nero was so vainglorious about his singing voice he had other singers whipped. I don't pity them. They knew signs, they who with the Greeks invented myth. Nero's ring portrayed Apollo flaying Marsyas. More fool them if they didn't heed. Lesser mortals wore rings engraved with images of temples, flowers or birds. *Signet/Cygnet*. There's a family of eight under the West Street Pier.

Notes

The Marseillaise : the quote is from Erik Satie's *Les Raisonnements d'un têtu*. (This and all other translations from the French are my own.)

Montparnasse—Rambouillet : the quote is from Alphonse Daudet's *Lettres de mon Moulin:* 'Les trois messes basses' ("Two truffled turkeys?— Yes, Reverend, two magnificent turkeys stuffed with truffles.").

His Letters Are in Pencil : *Marianne* is a national emblem of France. In modern times she is a symbol of Freedom, Equality and Fraternity. *Facteur: Journée du Timbre*: Postman: Day of the Stamp.

The Light-Bearer : when I was six, my older sister's boyfriend and his friend capsized in these waters and drowned. They were both seventeen years old.

What Men Did Not Read in Their Hearts : the title and the italicised pieces are quoted from The Decalogue: *Catechism of the Catholic Church*.

Nigg Bay, Aberdeen : *Katúsha Máslova* and *Nekhlúdov* are the protagonists in Leo Tolstoy's *Resurrection*.

Nazareth House : the poem alludes to Miss Havisham and the fire in Charles Dickens' *Great Expectations*. As an eighteen-year-old I worked for nine months as a Community Service Volunteer at the children's home Nazareth House, in Aberdeen. One of the working residents told me about the fire that had occurred when she was a child living there in Care, in which an adult had died. She said she had never recovered from being accused of starting the fire.

Loons & Quines : During the time I worked at Nazareth House, I made two formal statements about my suspicions of mental and physical abuse of some of the children I worked with. The first was in person to the Mother Superior, the second in a letter to Community Service Volunteers, to which I still have the reply. Both claimed to have investigated; both claimed to have found no evidence of abuse.

> In a symbolic trial in Aberdeen in 2000, one nun, known in her childcare days as Sister Alphonso [real name Marie Docherty], was convicted of cruel and unnatural treatment. And 40 nuns belonging to the Poor Sisters of Nazareth and the Daughters of Charity of St Vincent de Paul are named in a civil action by more than 500 people, mostly middle-aged or elderly, who are claiming compensation from the orders…

And the Poor Sisters aren't poor (the order has £154m in the bank)—they've been rebranded and they're simply Sisters. (*The Guardian*, 12 April 2003).

A Road in Berlin : the quote is from Dylan Thomas' poem 'The force that through the green fuse drives the flower' in *Collected Poems 1934–1952*.

Der Rote Stern Verlag : The Red Star Press. The book is *Mother Courage and Her Children* by Bertolt Brecht.

The MAFF, Whitehall : Ministry of Agriculture, Fisheries and Food, Whitehall Place, London. The poem alludes to *Novel on Yellow Paper* and *The Holiday* by Stevie Smith.

Christian Street, Whitechapel : the "small collection" is *Coin of the Tribute* by Sister Mary Teresita Heenan (Senate Books, 1976). The quote is the final quatrain of Victor Hugo's poem 'Demain, dès l'aube' ('Tomorrow at Dawn').

Aegean Sea : one phrase in each section is quoted from Sappho.

Που είναι ο φούρνος; means "Where is the bread shop?"

Cortège : the quote is from Sappho.

On the Highway : the quote is from Gary Snyder's poem 'Mountain Spirit' in *Mountains and Rivers Without End*.

Gordon Gardens: an attractive garden named after General Gordon and which houses his statue. Charles George Gordon (1833–1885), known as "Chinese Gordon", was a British army officer and administrator. He is remembered for his Campaigns in China and Northern Africa. Gordon lived and worked in Gravesend between 1865 and 1871 and during that time showed great generosity and kindness to the poor people of the borough.

Wodnesdaeg : *Hoodening* is an East Kent winter custom dating back many centuries. In its current form, a small band of villagers spend around four days before Christmas touring local pubs and private parties, performing a humorous play along the theme of death and resurrection, drinking a lot of beer, and collecting money for charity. A new play is written each year in rhyming couplets by one of the troupe, and references to recent events (local, national and international) are frequently included, although the setting is based on a ploughing team from the 19th century. My thanks to Dr. Ben Jones for his website information and for permission to quote from *Waggoner's Song*. The second quote is from Robert Louis Stevenson's *A Child's Garden of Verses:* 'Windy Nights'.

Lightning Source UK Ltd.
Milton Keynes UK
UKOW040701221012

200955UK00001B/24/P

9 781848 612242